Soda Glazing

D1290054

SODA GLAZING

Ruthanne Tudball

A & C Black · London

University of Pennsylvania Press · Philadelphia

First published in Great Britain 1995
A & C Black (Publishers) Limited
35 Bedford Row
London WC1R 4JH

ISBN 0 7136 3903 2

Published simultaneously in the US by:
University of Pennsylvania Press
423 Guardian Drive, Philadelphia, PA 19104

Reprinted 1996

ISBN 0 8122 1571 0
Copyright © 1995 Ruthanne Tudball

A CIP catalogue record for this book is available
from the British Library

All rights reserved. No part of this publication may
be reproduced in any form or by any means –
graphic, electronic or mechanical, including
photocopying, recording, taping or information
storage and retrieval systems – without the prior
permission in writing of the publishers.

Cover illustrations
front Ginger jar by Ruthanne Tudball, faceted,
black slip, 32 cm high.

back Plate with inlaid porcelain by Mima
Weissmann.

Frontispiece Bottle by Ruthanne Tudball, faceted,
30 cm high.

Filmset by August Filmsetting, St. Helens
Printed in Hong Kong by Wing King Tong Co. Ltd.

Contents

Dedication

To my family on both sides of the Atlantic.

Acknowledgements

This book is an attempt to give a practical guide to the basic concepts of soda glazing and to present some of the many and varied approaches of individual potters who are soda glazing throughout the world today.

I would like to thank all of the potters represented here who are actively involved in soda glazing for so generously providing information about their working methods and aesthetic approaches to making pots and firing them. Without them, this book would not have been possible.

Introduction

The use of salt (sodium chloride) to glaze various types of ceramic ware has a long and honourable tradition in the history of world ceramics, and many potters throughout the world today continue to produce fine salt-glazed ware. However, sodium chloride vapour is hazardous and produces pollution in the form of thick white clouds of dilute hydrochloric acid gas. Stringent pollution laws, particularly in urban areas, have encouraged many potters who want to pursue vapour glazing, but who are also very conscious of the possible environmental impact of sending unnecessary pollutants into the atmosphere, to seek an alternative. Large industrial potteries could install elaborate and expensive scrubbing devices to clean the discharge with a washing tower, but a more logical and simple approach for smaller scale studio potters has been to find a source of sodium vapour that avoids the production of hydrochloric acid gas in the first place.

Apart from avoiding the environmental impact of salt, soda has a subtle nature of its own in the way that it behaves when interacting with clay bodies and slips. Exploiting the special character of soda for its own sake perhaps should in the end take precedence over trying to achieve 'salt glaze' without salt.

There are several advantages in using soda apart from causing less wear and tear on the environment. It also causes less wear and tear on the kiln and kiln furniture. The vapour forms a non-reactive coating or 'crust' on the surface of the bricks rather than eating into them as rock salt does. It is also less corrosive to metal, and the colours produced tend to be brighter and softer.

It is possible to get almost identical results to salt glazing, if that is what you want. You can get the orange peel surface uniformly around the pot by several methods of introducing the soda into the kiln. Pots can be made to look just like their salty brothers and sisters, but they can also have a unique look of their own. Pots can be made to look very much like wood-fired pots with heavily glazed parts on one side and flashing on the other. There are many possibilities through varying clay bodies, slips, firing temperature, time span of soda introduction, firing atmosphere, amount of soda used, placing of pots, etc. These offer rich variation and enough possibilities to keep one going for a lifetime.

Chapter One

Soda Glazing: A Brief History

Nobody knows for sure how, why or exactly when salt glazing started, and as soda glazing derives from salt glazing, its history is equally vague. How did people get the idea to throw salt into a kiln to achieve a glazed surface on clay? There are many theories that include Roman and German methods for preserving foodstuffs in salt brine using vats in ovens. Over time the vats developed a glaze-like surface. Other theories speculate that kilns in the Rhineland were fired with salt-saturated driftwood or salt-saturated wooden boxes in which preserved meat or herring were transported. The Rhineland is too far inland for much, if any, driftwood to have been available. Maybe the idea for salt glazing came from the practice of combining silica and soda in glass making or maybe from the Middle East.

I am as uncertain as anybody else. However, having read some of the extensive research done by American Pamela Vandiver of the Smithsonian Institution into glazes and their constituents, it may not be an unreasonable hypothesis that the Middle East may be the missing link in providing a major source of inspiration for the beginning of vapour glazing in Germany.

German stoneware salt glazing of around the 13th century is a relatively

Left
A worker putting salt into a kiln in the Westerwald, Germany.

new process as compared to a method used during the Middle Kingdom in Egypt for Egyptian faience, which was being made around 4500 BC when the first truly ceramic body composition evolved in Egypt and Mesopotamia. Natron, a hydrous sodium carbonate found in desert deposits near the River Nile, was combined with the powder of crushed quartz pebbles and malachite ore containing copper to make a paste which was formed by hand or in moulds into simple shapes. During drying, the sodium solution migrated to the surface and an 'efflorescent' sodium layer was deposited. These shapes were very low-fired at about 900°C and the white quartz body became coated with a glaze from the sodium, made blue by the copper.

The white sodium scum that forms from efflorescence during drying on ceramic bodies which contain soluble salts is a defect for most pottery because it causes problems of glaze adherence. In the manufacture of Egyptian faience, however, the phenomenon was used positively as a source of surface glaze itself. Over time improvements in the technique introduced clay for workability combined with a less pure sand, and the pure quartz was used only as a slip.

Along with improvements in the body used for faience, a special variation of vapour glazing was sometimes used to fire Egyptian faience. Indeed, it is still

A crust forms on the walls of my soda kiln made of HT1 bricks.

centuries. 'Smear' glazing was also used in which an alkaline glaze composition (containing sodium) would be smeared over the inside of a closed clay saggar (a refractory clay box) containing unglazed ware so that when it vaporised during firing, it deposited vapour on the enclosed ware forming a thin adherent

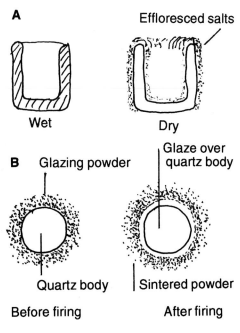

Methods of glazing Egyptian faience.
A) Efflorescence of sodium to surface, forming glaze when fired.
B) Cementation of glaze

employed today for the manufacture of Qom donkey beads in Iran. In this process a quartz-paste body is embedded in a powder mixture consisting of calcined lime, sodium carbonate, silica and charcoal with some copper for colouring. On heating to about 1000°C, the sodium carbonate diffuses to the quartz paste body/slip where it reacts, releasing sodium vapours which react with the silicate surface and form an alkali silicate glaze. The carbon in the surrounding glazing powder reduces the amount of CO_2 formed so that the process can continue to build up a glaze layer. As the first liquid is formed, it penetrates into the quartz powder and the bead simultaneously shrinks away from the surrounding powder to allow a shiny coating to be formed (see Kingery, p.277).

In Medieval Germany a related process was used when mineral salt was added to a kiln at a temperature of about 1200°C, and this became the standard method for fine English stoneware during the 17th and early 18th

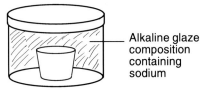

Smear method in closed clay saggar. A mixture containing sodium is smeared on the inside walls of a closed saggar. The sodium vapourises during firing and reacts with the enclosed clay ware and forms a glazed surface

porefree alkali-silicate glass coating.

How and why potters in Germany began putting mineral salts into kilns may never be known. But to conjecture for a minute, it could be that the knowledge of vapour glazing had spread from the Middle East and something as simple as the non-availability of natron caused potters to look for a simple and cheap substitute. As it is well-known that brine was widely used for preserving, salt was clearly easy to come by and may have been seen as an obvious substitute as an alkali source.

To conjecture still further, it could be that the Crusades were the missing link in the flow of information about sodium vapour glaze from Egypt to Germany. The Crusades were a series of European military expeditions directed against Muslim control of Jerusalem and the Christian shrine of the Holy Sepulchre which took place from 1095 to 1270. Germany was deeply involved in the Crusades and the movement of thousands of crusaders between Europe and especially Germany and Egypt seems an obvious vehicle for the transportation of artefacts and information. Who knows? There may have been some very perceptive potters amongst the crusaders who may have put the notion of sodium vapour glazing together with the easy availability of stoneware clays suitable for high temperature salt glaze in the Rhine valley, and 'eureka', they may have learned something that revolutionised German pottery making when they ventured so far from home.

However it began, salt glazing flourished in the Rhineland from the 13th through to the 15th centuries, especially in the vicinity of Cologne. About 1690 the Brothers Elers, who were of German origin, introduced salt glazing into England at Royal Doulton.

Typical orange peel surface obtained in a soda firing.

Of course, the Europeans were great colonisers of the rest of the world and took their knowledge with them, especially to the American Colonies of Carolina, up to Canada, and to Bendigo, Australia.

Salt glazing continued until, in an attempt to improve the infamous pea soup fogs of London and other large cities in the 1950s, stringent pollution laws shut down salt kilns, (including Doultons of Lambeth) in urban areas. Similar laws were enacted in the early 1970s in the United States. Anyone wanting to pursue salt glazing had to move into the country, away from other sources of urban pollution, where the white clouds of dilute hydrochloric acid gas coming from the salt kilns would go relatively unnoticed.

Warren Mather's 'Reading Matter', soda glazed.

With ever-growing concern about pollution, potters in many parts of the world have tried to find an acceptable alternative to salt for vapour glazing. This material has to be cheap, non-polluting and produce acceptable results. Sodium compounds other than salt are wide ranging in availability (and therefore price) and in efficiency in forming a glaze on ceramic work. The most universally available and cheapest sources of sodium, apart from salt, are sodium carbonate (Na_2CO_3 or soda ash), sodium bicarbonate ($NaHCO_3$ or baking soda) and borax ($Na_2B_4O_7 \cdot 10H_2O$).

In 1974 at Alfred University, New York, Jeff Zamek did his postgraduate thesis on 'Sodium Carbonate Vapor Firing' in an attempt to find a non-polluting method of vapour glazing that would produce a satisfactory and repeatable glaze finish and a method that was both 'physically and economically feasible for the studio potter'. The study was pivotal in producing evidence that it was possible to obtain the classic orange peel effect and flashing (hitherto obtained only from salt) with alternative non-chlorine sodium compounds. About four years later, Warren Mather and Bernice Hillman working at the Radcliffe Pottery Studio in Concorde, Massachusetts were successfully soda glazing in an urban environment and they published their working methods in *The Studio Potter*, 'Salt in the City: The Sodium Carbonate Solution'. Soda glazing had arrived as a viable alternative to salt glazing.

Left
Doulton's of Lambeth factory 1874. Ewer salt-glazed with relief decoration.
Victoria and Albert Museum, London.

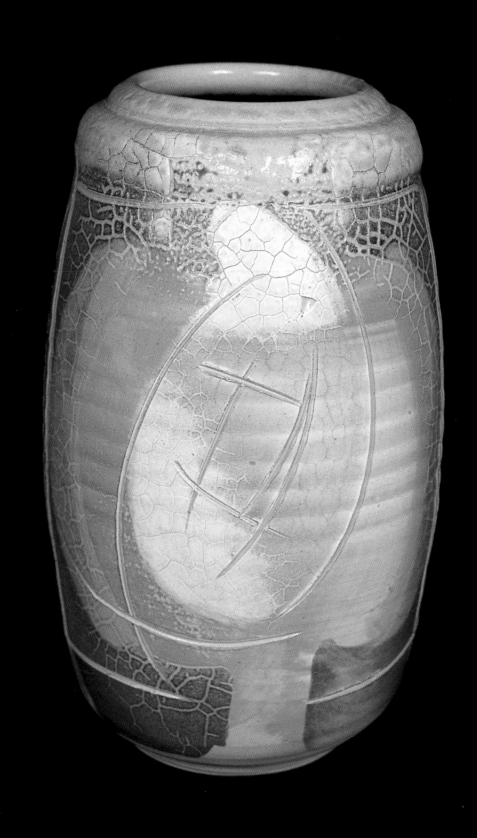

Chapter Two
Clays and Colour

Soda-glazed pots are fired in a kiln in the conventional way, but they need not be glazed and need not be biscuit-fired. Pots can be put into the kiln in the raw state and glazing will occur in the kiln when sodium is introduced, most commonly at around 1260°C (cone 8) when stoneware clay is beginning to vitrify. The sodium unites with the alumina and silica in the clay to produce a glaze, sodium alumino-silicate.

All clays contain silica, the glass-forming element, and alumina, the refractory element. The ratio of alumina to silica varies from clay to clay, and it is this ratio which affects the glaze finish. The higher the proportion of silica to alumina, the more sodium is attracted to the clay body, and the thicker the glaze formed. If the body or the slip covering the body is high in alumina, the sodium is resisted and a more matt, flashed surface tends to result.

Flashing is a colour response which tends towards a blush or a definite flame pattern across the clay in colours ranging from brilliant oranges, pinks and yellows to deeper reds and violets. It is caused by soda vapours coming into contact with substances on the clay's surface.

In a report published in 1948 by Borax Consolidated Ltd in the USA,

studies of the relationship between the alumina: silica ratio, iron content in the clay and firing temperature were cited in an effort to produce better quality salt-glazed sewer pipes and sanitary ware and to reduce the proportion of defective products for industry.

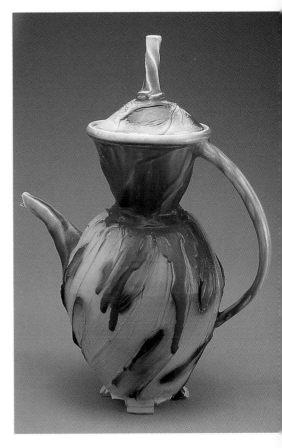

Left
Blossom Jar by Gail Nichols, height 36 cm.
Photograph by Ian Whatman

Tea server by Jay Lacouture, $18\frac{1}{2} \times 7 \times 9\frac{1}{2}$ in. Soda vapour glazed porcelain.

Vase by Christopher Staley, 22″ high.
Thrown, faceted porcelain, soda glazed.

The earlier studies by Baringer and Mackler (1902 and 1905) and a later study by Schurecht (1923), which were cited in the Stevens and Cossey 1948 study, have led to the conclusion that the best silica/alumina ratio in a clay body for salting is about 5 : 1. This is a good starting point for experimentation.

The iron content of clay will affect the colour response quite dramatically. Iron will resist sodium, and depending on the amount of iron in the body the colour will vary from a white to pale tan in clays containing 0–2% iron to a deep mahogany brown to metallic black/brown when over 8%. Schurecht found that in order to develop a clay body that had a colour and glaze finish acceptable to industrial standards, the amount of iron oxide in a clay body had to be

strictly controlled. He found that reducing the iron oxide content of a clay body fired at 1145°C by 1% would be equivalent to the addition of 7.8% silica, while the same reduction in iron in a body fired at 1210°C would be equivalent to adding 12.6% silica and thereby would obtain a brighter glaze.

The only way to discover what all this theory means in practice is to test clay bodies that are high in iron, high in silica, high in alumina and various combinations of these to find the clay body with the colour response you require for your particular aesthetic satisfaction. Many clay supply companies publish chemical analysis tables for all the clays they sell and in my experience they are usually very helpful in answering technical questions about clays.

The sodium glaze itself has no colour, and it takes various shades from the clay beneath. Many potters use slips and/or oxides and stains to introduce colour on to the surface of their pots, and depending on the atmosphere in which the pots are fired and the amount of sodium used, colour response will vary greatly. If glazes are used, they will be affected by the fluxing action of the soda. The colour and texture of the glaze can change quite dramatically when hit by sodium vapour (because soda is a flux, it is like adding an extra flux to the glaze mix, thereby lowering the eutectic point of the glaze). Copper glazes will turn bluish in an oxidised atmosphere and reddish when reduced. Iron-bearing glazes such as tenmokus tend to be bleached to various tones of green. Chrome oxide colours can become quite intensified toward yellow-green and chartreuse. The extra fluxing action can make some glazes run down the pot, but some, such as magnesia matts and some

Above
Extra fluxing action with soda on bowls by
Wayne Fuerst, Radcliffe Ceramics Studio.

Below
Carbon trapping appears as black dappling on
this faceted jar, 6 in. high by Ruthanne
Tudball.

Heavy soda on high iron body.

Flashing.

High silica porcelain body attracts more soda.

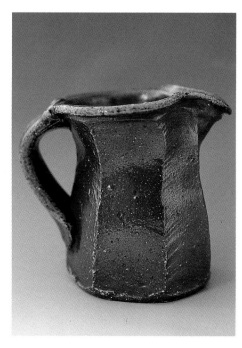

High iron body resists soda and becomes metallic.

High alumina slip resists soda and encourages oranges.

Carbon trapping looks like a grey smokey surface on this porcelain.

barium matt glazes, will crystallise and can form dry, rough patches.

You can get a very shiny, sometimes crazed, surface with soda glazing, and for some this is acceptable, but it can be a problem for others. It is possible to add mattness enhancers (alumina, iron, titanium) to the clay itself or just to the surface in the form of slips or matt glazes if you wish to lose the characteristic orange peel texture.

'Carbon trapping' is another effect which can add interest and variety to the glazed surface, but it can also be very unpleasant and can block out any colour on surfaces if overdone. It is a phenomenon which occurs particularly in sodium glazes during early reduction prior to the sealing of the clay surface by the 'glassification' of fluxes. The porous clay and perhaps also the highly receptive soluble sodium itself can trap the carbon present in the reducing atmosphere and this later appears as 'smokey' shadows or Dalmatian-type spots within the glaze.

Chapter Three
Kilns and Firing

Any fossil fuel burning kiln can be used for soda glazing. I have even successfully experimented with soda glazing in sealed saggars in an electric kiln, although for potting on a large scale, this is impractical as sodium introduced directly into an electric kiln chamber will destroy the metal elements.

A sprung arch kiln with a 1 m³ chamber is said to be the most efficient for heat distribution and even firing, but as even the most efficient kilns have their quirks, it is almost impossible to say one is any better than another.

Many potters wanting to soda glaze have experimented with different types of kilns trying to find the optimum method of distributing soda throughout the chamber. One way is to buy burners which will allow you to introduce your sodium source through the burner itself (see Martin Goerg's burners on page 41).

Left
John Teiser's round kiln has many bung holes for flexibility in introducing soda.

Above
Group of Planters by John Teiser, tallest 21 inches, smallest 4½ inches.

High alumina wads lift pots off the kiln shelf to prevent sticking. Radcliffe Ceramics Studio kiln.

Another more popular method is to build the kiln so that it has numerous bungholes around it so that the soda can be introduced from all sides of the chamber. Another way is to build a kiln that has a shape which will aid in the distribution of the soda, say, a round kiln, for instance, with burners pointed along the wall so that the vapour will swirl around the chamber.

John Teiser of Ross-on-Wye, Hereford, England has built a round kiln specifically with soda glazing in mind. The round kiln eliminates corners into which the vapour is less likely to penetrate. The fireboxes enter at a tangent to the bagwall to create a circular swirling effect with an anti-clockwise bias so that any effect of the earth's rotation will be working with rather than against the rotation of the kiln atmosphere (known as the Coriolis Effect). As John lives in the northern hemisphere the bias is opposite to that for anyone living in the southern hemisphere. There are about 20 ports around the kiln at all levels to allow for maximum flexibility for trying different methods of introducing soda to all parts of the kiln.

Traditionally, pots to be sodium vapour glazed are put into the kiln raw and once-fired, integrating the making and firing processes without the interruption and extra expense of biscuit firing. The initial part of the firing will be slow to take the pots through the biscuit stage. If the pots are biscuit-fired, of course, this stage can be passed through quite quickly. The raw or biscuited pots are usually placed on small dough-like wads made of a 3 : 1 mixture of alumina hydrate and china clay to lift the pots up to prevent the soda glaze sticking them to the kiln shelves.

After soaking the kiln for about one hour at 900°C to burn out any carbonaceous matter to avoid any possible bloating, a reducing atmosphere can be maintained to convert the ferric oxide compounds in the body and in slips to the ferrous state. In this condition the surface becomes more glassy, the body denser and less porous and a better soda glaze is produced. It is good practice to oxidise for about 30 minutes at about 1150°C to avoid carbon trapping (trapping black/grey carbon molecules in the glaze) when the sodium already present in the kiln is beginning to vaporise and to seal the body, and then maintain only a light reduction or neutral atmosphere throughout the rest of the firing.

It is certainly possible to soda glaze at low temperatures (1000°–1200°C) but the results are more likely to be flashed with the vapours rather than achieving an orange peel effect although borax or boric oxide added to the soda compound will help to achieve a thicker glaze at lower temperatures.

When stoneware clays are used, soda is introduced to the kiln at about 1260°C (cone 8) through to 1300°C (cone 10). One of the important things to remember about using soda compounds other than salt is that they break down in the kiln much more slowly than salt. To compensate for this slower reaction, soda can be introduced in small amounts over a fairly long period for 2–3 hours if you want a reasonably even, overall glaze

Dish fired to cone 1, soda glazed by Amy Woods, Radcliffe Ceramics Studio.

Above
Val Nicholls taking a test ring out of her kiln.
Photograph by Audrey Hutchinson

Left
Test rings are pulled from the kiln to help
assess the build-up of soda on the clay body.

covering. Putting larger amounts of soda in the kiln over a short period will tend to produce 'one-sided' pots with a heavy glaze on one side and starved of soda on the other, or it will be just flashed, much as in wood-firing.

It is common practice to put test rings in a soda kiln near a spy hole so they can be pulled out on a wire at intervals throughout the period of soda being introduced to help give some indication of how much soda covering has taken place on the body. These test rings are simply coils of clay formed into rings about $1\frac{1}{4}$ in (3 cm) in diameter and flattened on one side to enable them to stand upright. They should be made of the same clay as the work in the kiln. I dip the top of each ring in a dark slip which helps me to see more easily the action of the soda.

John Teiser uses small straight-sided pots with a small looped handle over the top (about 4 in or 10 cm in all) instead of test rings, because he feels that using rings alone can give inaccurate information. The ring handle on top can be well glazed while the body of the small pot is quite dry, thus indicating that this may be the same for the larger pots in the kiln.

An oxidising soak at the end of the firing will oxidise any metallic iron particles back to ferric oxide. This will give the warmer oranges from iron-bearing bodies and slips.

A typical firing in my kiln, which has 18 cu.ft. of packing space and is built of High Thermal Insulation Bricks (HTI 23) after three courses of heavy refractory bricks in the fireboxes, goes as follows:

● Night before firing both gas burners are put on very low. The primary air is open and the damper is fully open.
● 7.30 am – the kiln is at about 350–

450°C. I turn up the burners slightly.

- 9.30–10 am usually by now 600°C has been reached and I can turn up the burners.
- By about 11 am 850–900°C has been reached and I soak the kiln for about 1 hour.
- After the soak, the primary air is turned down, the burners are turned up and the damper is put partially in so that there is only a light reduction.
- This continues until the pyrometer reads 1150°C when I oxidise for half an hour. Then I put the damper in about 4 in (10 cm) so the temperature continues to rise and the atmosphere is neutral to light reduction.

I spray soda solution through the burner ports.

- When cone 8 is bending over, I open the damper and begin to spray soda into the fireboxes over the tops of the burners (I do not have a lot of spraying points around the kiln). Sometimes I waft the damper to create turbulence in the kiln. The soda is sprayed in small amounts about every 15 minutes over 2–3 hours.
- When the soda is finished, cone 9 is usually flat, but I do not depend on the cones only as they will give a false reading once the soda begins to flux them. The pyrometer will indicate if the temperature is constant, rising or falling, and the colour of the kiln atmosphere along with the cones and the draw rings will let me know when the firing is complete. The draw rings

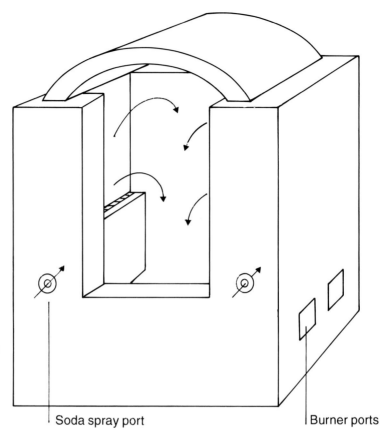

Kiln used by John Chalke and Barbara Tipton. A fairly typical sprung arch down-draught kiln with soda spray ports built into it for spraying along the fireboxes over the burners.

Soda spray port

Burner ports

tell me fairly well how much soda has accumulated on the pots.

- I soak the kiln at top temperature for 1–1½ hours until cone 10 is flat.
- The kiln is fast cooled with the damper and all bungs out to about 950°C. Then I clam it up and wait two days to let it continue cooling.

The soda solution is not measured, but I add enough boiling water to a generous handful of bicarbonate of soda to make a super-saturated solution i.e. when I pour the mixture into the sprayer through a 200s mesh sieve, there is a very small amount left at the bottom of the jug. This is not very scientific but it works. When the kiln was new I used about 3 kg of soda. Now I use about 1½ kg or less.

John Teiser's Kiln

John Teiser's kiln is 49 in (124 cm) in diameter and has a wall height of 49 in (124 cm) with a rise to the top of the dome of 12 in (30.5 cm) giving it an overall volume of about 60 cu.ft.

The walls are built of an inner skin of Nettle 42 heavy fibrebrick (42% alumina), backed up with another skin of seconds quality 1400°C HTI bricks. The heavy bricks are circle bricks with 20 forming a complete circle 48 in (122 cm) in diameter without mortar joints (mortar adds an extra inch). The outer HTIs were cut to fit around the inner wall but the inner and outer skins were not tied together because of differing expansion rates. A panel of 2 in

John Teiser's kiln is 49 in. (125 cm) in diameter and has a wall height of 49 in. (125 cm) with a rise on the top of the dome of 12 in. (305 mm) giving it an overall volume of about 60 cubic feet.

Section through A–B on plan

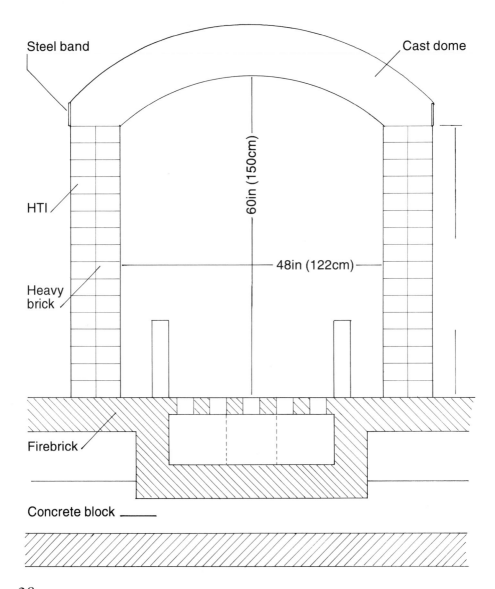

Steel band

Cast dome

HTI

Heavy brick

60in (150cm)

48in (122cm)

Firebrick

Concrete block _____

Plan of John Teiser's kiln.

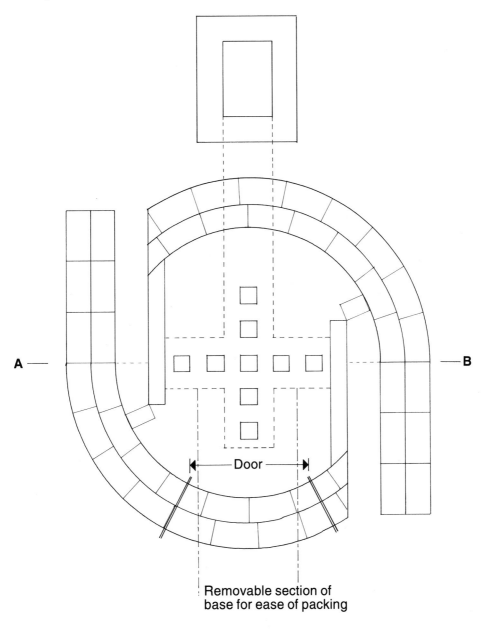

A — — — B

Door

Removable section of
base for ease of packing

John Teiser's Kiln. Flues and arches.

Below
Bung holes.

Right
The dome.

(5 cm) weldmesh is wrapped around the kiln to give extra support with a removable section for the door. When the door section is bolted into place, the whole panel is pulled tight.

The dome was cast in a single piece *in situ*. To make a former to cast over, a piece of chipboard was cut to a 49 in (124 cm) circle with one straight edge. This was supported on four legs of 4×2 timber so that the top surface was flush with the top of the wall. The straight edge was positioned across the doorway. A second piece of chipboard shaped, like a dovetail, was cut to fit the doorway, butting up to the straight side of the circular piece and supported on two legs with wedges under them.

Soft red building sand with about 10% powdered clay was added and moistened until it held together in a firm lump when squeezed in the hand. This mixture was heaped onto the chipboard and thoroughly compacted with a wooden mallet. A curved plywood template was used to shape the mound into a smooth dome. This was covered with damp newspaper to separate the sand former from the casting mix. A steel band, 4 in (10 cm) wide and $\frac{1}{4}$ in (7 mm) thick, that had been rolled into two semicircles by a local engineering firm, was placed on the outer edge of the wall to act as shuttering for the casting mix and support for the finished dome.

Planter by John Teiser, 6 in high, 10 inches wide with brushed slip of 50/50 SMD ball clay and kaolin.

The recipe for the casting mix is based on recommendations in an article in the American periodical, *The Studio Potter*, by Richard Leach. The materials John used (all measured by volume not weight) are as follows:

First 5 mixes: This mix is directly pounded onto the compacted sand former. This inner layer has a higher alumina content to provide a more durable, finer and more densely packed inner skin.

Fireclay	2 parts
Grog 8–25s	1 part
Grog 30s–dust	1 part
Alumina	1 part
Portland cement	1 part
Vermiculite	1 part

Remaining 10 mixes: The remaining mix is more coarse with less alumina and acts as an outer insulating layer.

Fireclay	2 parts
Smashed firebrick (up to 1 in/2.5 cm)	
Grog 8–25s	$\frac{1}{2}$ part
Grog 30s-dust	$\frac{1}{2}$ part
Alumina	1 part
Portland cement	1 part
Vermiculite	1 part
Sawdust	1 part

These were mixed in a concrete mixer with one 5 litre measure of water. After the mix hardened, the wedges were knocked out from under the two legs holding up the dovetail-shaped piece of chipboard in the doorway. Then the front two legs supporting the large circular piece of chipboard were notched with a saw and broken with a long pole. The chipboard and sand collapsed neatly into the kiln leaving the dome in place. The sand was simply shovelled out. The Romans used a similar method for building domes and arches but they used

earth to fill the whole building.

The main underfloor flue is 9 × 9 in (23 cm × 23 cm), and the chimney is 9 × 12 in (23 cm × 30.5 cm) with a height of 12.5 feet (3.8 m) above the level of the chamber floor. This gives more draught than is needed for the blower-fed oil burners, but it is very useful when burning wood in the early stages of the firing to heat the fireboxes. A kiln batt, inserted across the flue between the chamber and the chimney, is used as a damper.

Fireboxes are 9 in (23 cm) high and 9 in (23 cm) across (changed from 6 in (15 cm)) and are bridged by slabs cast in Durax C1600 (50% alumina). Small flame ramps are placed at the ends to deflect the flame upwards at about 45°.

Shelves are rectangular with one corner knocked off to fit the round wall. The burners are based on those described by Dennis Parks in his book, *A Potter's Guide to Raw Glazing and Oil Firing* but with modifications to make them more efficient in vaporising the heavy waste oil.

Jack Doherty's Kiln

Jack Doherty's kiln.

Jack Doherty wanted a kiln that would be economical to fire with propane, economical to build (just in case his experiments with soda firing did not work), small enough to use for experimentation in introducing soda compounds and achieving an acceptably even distribution of vapour within the chamber, but big enough to produce a reasonable quantity of pots.

Using Jack Troy's recipes from his experiments in homemade insulating castables as detailed in his book on salt glazing, Jack Doherty used readily available materials i.e. fireclay, grog, sawdust, vermiculite, alumina and cement, to make his own castable.

He found that vermiculite in the mix

Jack compacting castable for kiln arch.

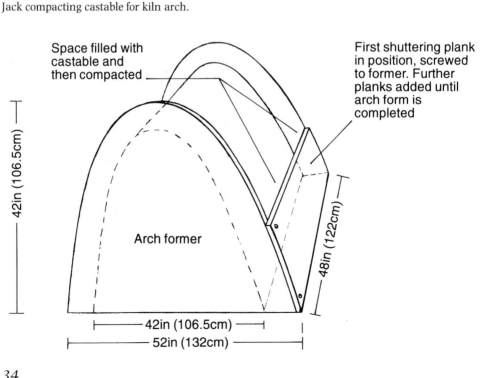

Space filled with castable and then compacted

First shuttering plank in position, screwed to former. Further planks added until arch form is completed

42in (106.5cm)

Arch former

48in (122cm)

42in (106.5cm)

52in (132cm)

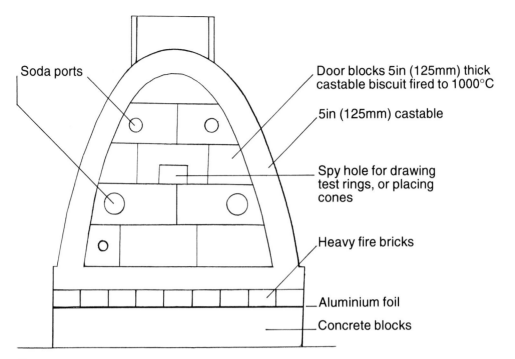

Soda ports

Door blocks 5in (125mm) thick castable biscuit fired to 1000°C

5in (125mm) castable

Spy hole for drawing test rings, or placing cones

Heavy fire bricks

Aluminium foil

Concrete blocks

Front

Back

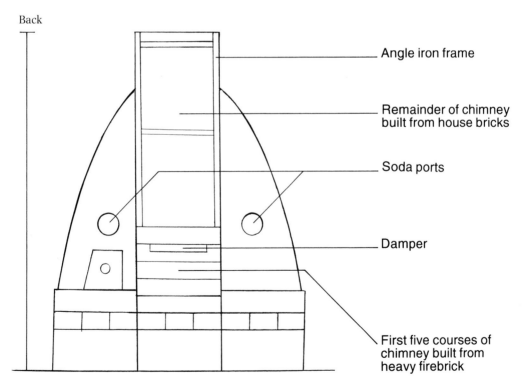

Angle iron frame

Remainder of chimney built from house bricks

Soda ports

Damper

First five courses of chimney built from heavy firebrick

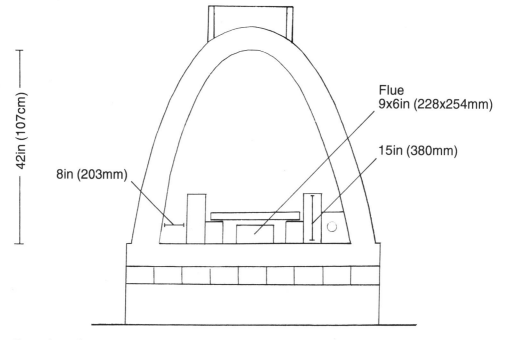

Flue
9x6in (228x254mm)

15in (380mm)

8in (203mm)

Front, through view

Plan view

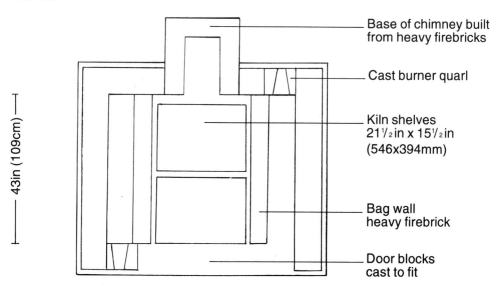

Base of chimney built
from heavy firebricks

Cast burner quarl

Kiln shelves
21½in x 15½in
(546x394mm)

Bag wall
heavy firebrick

Door blocks
cast to fit

caused the castable to crumble, scattering debris into the pots. His final recipe was (by volume):

Fireclay	2 parts
Sawdust	2 parts (mixture of fine sawdust and wood chippings)
Grog	2 parts (divided between three grades i.e. dust to $\frac{3}{8}$in (5 mm)
Alumina	$\frac{1}{2}$ part
Cement	$\frac{1}{2}$ part

Using a wooden former, this mixture was used to cast an 18 cu. ft. downdraught catenary arch kiln with six soda ports (four in the front and two in back). The catenary arch is 5 in (12.5 cm) thick and is covered with $1\frac{1}{2}$ in (4 cm) of ceramic fibre offcuts (acquired free) stapled onto a wire mesh.

This kiln fires extremely evenly using Aeromatic Barter FR100 burners firing from opposite sides. There is less than $\frac{1}{2}$ cone difference between top and bottom, front and back. The only sign of wear and tear after two years is in the fireboxes opposite the direction of the flame. Jack uses high alumina castable to repair this.

There is a zirconium-based non-vitreous coating which can be obtained that prevents the soda from settling on and reacting with the bricks. John Teiser has coated the hot face walls of his kiln with this and Martin Goerg uses something similar to protect the inside of his kiln. In England this substance is called Furnacecote Non-Vit.

Chapter Four

Introducing Soda into the Kiln

All soda glazers have their own pet ways of introducing soda into their kilns to get the results they want from their vapour firing.

There are several ways to get soda into a kiln, and it is only through experimentation that the most efficient method can be found for your own particular aesthetic goals.

Methods

Angle iron

Small amounts of the sodium can be put into the channel of a piece of angle iron and introduced into the fireboxes from a port above the burners. The dampened soda is dropped through the flames into the firebox where it will slowly vaporise. This is repeated every 5–10 minutes until the soda is finished.

Left
Faceted teabowl with orange slip and willow ash trailing 6 inches high by Ruthanne Tudball.

Above
Gail Nichols adding soda mix into her kiln's fireboxes on angle iron.

'Packages' of soda

Small amounts of soda can be wrapped in newspaper or paper towel (some people use aluminium foil) and dropped into the fireboxes as close to the hottest part of the flame as possible. Do not use high quality magazine paper because there is too much china clay in the paper and it does not burn as quickly.

Mix soda with volatile additions

In soda packages, the soda can be mixed with sawdust or wood shavings to introduce more moisture and also to increase temperatures in the fireboxes (as will oil or powdered coal or other materials) to help to volatilise the soda. Incidentally this will help to create a reduction atmosphere in the kiln at the same time.

Containers in kiln

Put small amounts of soda into small fired pots placed throughout the kiln near the ware as is done with salt in the LaBorne kilns in Central France.

Spray soda into kiln

Using an air compressor and a water tank, soda can be mixed with water and sprayed into the kiln as a mist. The amount of soda that will go into solution varies, depending on the temperature of the water, e.g. from about 250 g ($\frac{1}{2}$ lb) per gallon at 32°F to as much as $1\frac{1}{2}$ kg (3 lb) per gallon at 100° F. *Note:* A drop in temperature of the solution can cause soda crystals to form and block the spray mechanism. This can usually be cleared by heating the orifice or washing it through with hot water.

A pressurised garden sprayer can also be used to spray a hot soda solution into the kiln. However, if it is plastic, care must be taken not to get it too close to the flames. Spraying water into a kiln is potentially dangerous because of rapid build up of steam pressure inside the kiln if too much water is introduced at one time. I never use more than 1 litre over 4–5 minutes and have never experienced any problems.

Spraying a fine mist directly onto pots through ports around the kiln is a simple way to get soda to all parts of the kiln without heavy glaze build-up in one area.

Other methods for introducing soda include using a converted grit gun to propel dampened soda into the kiln chamber. It can also be introduced through the blowers on some burners.

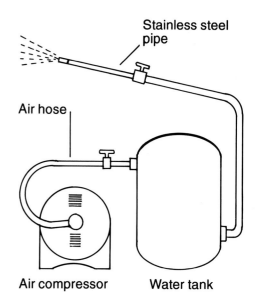

Stainless steel pipe

Air hose

Air compressor   Water tank

Val Nicholls spraying soda solution into her kiln with simple garden sprayer.
Photograph by Audrey Hutchinson

John Chalke and Barbara Tipton use a simple $2\frac{1}{2}$ gallon (11.36 litres) pressurised garden sprayer similar to the one I use.

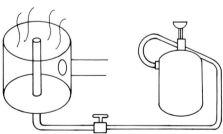

A tube is fitted through the base so that the injector reaches the top of the burner

Garden pump sprayer (3 Bar. pressure)

Martin Goerg injects his soda through specially adapted burners.

41

Barbara Tipton spraying into her kiln wearing welding goggles to protect her eyes from being damaged by the bright heat.

Common sources of sodium

Sodium chloride   NaCl (common salt)

When salt is heated, chlorine gas and dilute hydrochloric acid are released into the atmosphere. Sodium chloride literally explodes when it is introduced into the kiln at high temperatures because it is tied up with chlorine gas. It is this 'explosion' which breaks the sodium bonds and spreads the vapours throughout the kiln. In *Ceramic Science for the Potter*, W.G. Lawrence explains the reactions that go on when damp NaCl is introduced into a hot kiln as follows:

1. $2NaCl + 2H_2O \rightarrow 2NaOH + 2HCl\uparrow$
   The salt reacts with the water vapor present in the kiln atmosphere to form sodium hydroxide and hydrochloric acid gas which are given off in the surrounding atmosphere.
2. $4NaOH + Heat \rightarrow 2Na_2O + 2H_2O\uparrow$
   The sodium hydroxide formed in reaction 1 at the kiln temperature decomposes to form sodium oxide, Na_2O, and water vapour which is evolved.

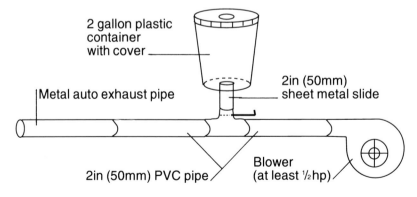

2 gallon plastic container with cover

Metal auto exhaust pipe

2in (50mm) sheet metal slide

2in (50mm) PVC pipe

Blower (at least ½hp)

Jay Lecouture blows a mixture of soda and sawdust into his kiln using an injector system he built himself.

3. $2Na_2O + xAl_2O_3 \cdot xSiO_2 \rightarrow 2Na_2O \cdot xAl_2O_3 \cdot xSiO_2$

   The sodium oxide reacts with the surface of the clay ware to form a sodium-alumina-silicate glaze.

Sodium carbonate Na_2CO_3 (soda ash/washing soda)

Sodium carbonate melts at 851°C and breaks down above 1000°C to give sodium oxide and carbon dioxide.

Sodium hydrogen carbonate (sodium bicarbonate or baking soda)

This decomposes readily and completely into sodium carbonate, carbon dioxide and water at 100°C and above.

Borax $Na_2B_4O_7 \cdot 10H_2O$

Borax added to whatever sodium compound is being used for glazing can brighten the colours, smooth the glaze finish, assist in achieving good glazes at temperatures up to about 80°C lower than sodium alone, and increases resistance to water penetration into a clay body.

Most soda products can be bought at your local supermarket in small amounts, but for bulk buying, pottery suppliers may be able to get them for you. I get mine from a wholesale chemical supply company. ICI sells bicarb as an animal feed additive, sold under the trade name 'Alkacarb'.

The environment

No alternative to salt is completely free of polluting emissions. Sodium carbonate and sodium bicarbonate produce very small amounts of CO_2 as a by-product. But the combustion products from the burners or the wood used to fire a kiln are likely to have much more significance in producing CO_2. Carbon dioxide is believed to contribute to global warming.

To get some perspective, here are some comparisons:

An adult breathing: It is estimated that the amount of CO_2 given off every 24 hours from the lungs of an average adult is between 700 and 1150 grams.

Sodium carbonate: One kilo of Na_2CO_3 will give off 415 grams of CO_2.

Sodium bicarbonate: One kilo of Bi-carb will give off 524 grams of CO_2.

Salt (sodium chloride): One kilo of NaCl will produce 600 grams of hydrochloric acid gas. If all of this 600 grams of gas were to be neutralised by using calcium carbonate (chalk), it would produce 360 grams of CO_2.

Natural gas (methane, CH_4), which is the cleanest burning fuel that a potter is likely to use, produces 44 grams of CO_2 for every 16 grams of methane burnt. In a 24-hour firing in a one cubic metre kiln, which uses around 5000 cubic feet of gas, 319 kg of carbon dioxide will be produced.

A small amount of sodium hydroxide (caustic soda) may go up the chimney and either be deposited on the cooler upper walls of the chimney or be exhausted. Any sodium hydroxide particles emitted from the kiln will immediately combine with carbon dioxide in the moist air and drop to the ground in close proximity to the kiln. Unless a large excess of Na_2CO_3 is used, these emissions are likely to be very small indeed. If there are green trees or plants near your kiln and they are not turning yellow, you can be fairly confident that the amount of sodium carbonate dropping to the ground is quite trivial.

Chapter Five
Individual potters and their working methods

Margaret Bohls

Margaret Bohls from Baton Rouge, Louisiana, USA, switched to soda after firing with salt. Apart from the obvious environmental advantages of using soda, she finds soda provides much nicer flashing and directional variation around the pots than her previous salt firings.

She says that she tries to achieve flowing forms that deal with natural imagery and patterns such as leaves, spirals or waves. She creates stable, regular forms and patterns and then alters the stability by perhaps changing the axis on which the pot sits or altering the flow of the lip.

Margaret uses a combination of glazes with the bare clay body using methods of resist (or masking of areas) to allow the glazes to be changed when they are hit by the soda, causing them to break and run together, again altering the stability and regularity of the patterns and creating a richer, more varied surface.

All of her pots are biscuit fired. The soda kiln is a 45 cu.ft. downdraught sprung arch kiln built completely of hard brick with two 500,000 BTU Eclipse burners with natural draught entering from the rear or the kiln. Firings take about 18 hours. A typical firing starts at 6 pm with both burners on low with the damper open about three inches. The burners are turned up slightly every hour until about 11 pm. By morning the kiln has reached dull red heat. She slowly opens the damper until cone 08 or 06 is reached. The damper and the primary air are left fully open throughout the rest of the firing, closing the damper a few inches only if the top to bottom temperature becomes uneven. The gas is turned up to about $\frac{3}{4}$ pressure which is enough to finish the firing. Margaret fires until cone 10 is flat and cone 11 is beginning to bend.

The soda is introduced at cone 8 two or three times on the half hour. About

Left
Coffee pot with melitta filter by Margaret Bohls, height 10 inches.

Right
Handled flower vase by Margaret Bohls, height 12 inches.

$\frac{1}{2}$ lb (227 g) is put into each of the two soda ports, each time using an angle iron until about 3–4 lb ($1\frac{1}{2}$–2 kg) of soda is used. The kiln reaches temperature about one hour after the final measure of soda is introduced. The soda ports are at the front of the kiln on either side of the door above and outside of the bagwall.

Firing with no reduction to body or glazes keeps her colours bright and clean. Reduction, she says, muddies her colours and causes her clay body to be too dark.

Teapot by Joan Bruneau, soda-fired white stoneware, cone 10.

Joan Bruneau

Joan Bruneau from Nova Scotia, Canada, was introduced to soda fired porcellanous stoneware by Sarah Coote while studying at the Nova Scotia College of Art and Design (1986–88).

Joan uses thrown elements to construct her pots, and the soda glazing process enhances the constructed character of the pots by emphasising seams and other marks of making.

The work is gas fired to cone 10 in an oxidation atmosphere. Approximately 7 lb (3.5 kg) of sodium bicarbonate is introduced into the kiln when cone 9 is

Dessert cup and spoon, soda-fired porcelain by Joan Bruneau.

bending. The soda is rolled into packets of moistened paper towels like eggrolls and introduced through side ports two at a time every 10 to 15 minutes. The gas pressure may be reduced and the damper shut about $\frac{3}{4}$ to allow the soda time to circulate and to prolong the sodium vapour action in the kiln. After the soda intervals have been completed, the damper is opened and gas is turned back up to clear the atmosphere. This is repeated about five or six times. When the soda introduction is complete, the damper is opened at least $\frac{3}{4}$, and the kiln has an oxidised soak for at least 45 minutes or until cone 10 is bending.

John Chalke and Barbara Tipton

John Chalke is a potter of many parts and keeping to one form of glazing is not his style, but he and his partner Barbara

Tipton vapour glaze when the clay body being used appears to them to demand the treatment of soda. John explains their methods.

> Looking back at all the glazing with salt that I ever did, I now find that material rather heavy-handed in its fluxing action, and unnecessarily demanding compared to glazing with soda. Soda is kinder to the kiln, to its surroundings, and to my own psyche. It dances, hesitates, varies. Constantly subtle. Compared to soda, salt is a bombast, a demander, not pleasantly inquisitive, but insistent. The other side of the coin is visible also, however. Soda needs extra coaxing and encouragement to get to those far-off places. All my soda firings used to hinge on a continuous and intense

47

'Good Horse/Bad Horse' coffee pot, soda vapour glaze over slip decoration, height 10 inches by Barbara Tipton.

30-minute period that happened one cone short of my intended one. Lately and simply I've extended that period to one hour and found a better distribution within the kiln as a result. The extra hour, plus a particular way of spraying vapour and pausing, has led to a more smoothed-out surface, an interesting neutral atmosphere and better penetration of shadowy areas.

A long wood flame, such as pine, really helps too to flow soda vapour along and through. Liquid propane gas, on the other hand, is difficult. Natural gas flame length is somewhere in between. With a somewhat open path, with special attention to kiln posts and taller or blockier pots which can deflect vapour away, usually I can now achieve an 80–90% success rate.

Pitcher by John Chalke, height 29 cm.

If I want the orange-peel surface, I use a shorter spray cycle plus no soak at the end. A 15-minute soak won't make much difference, but 30–45 minutes will. (One has to build this time into the firing schedule, otherwise the temperature may rise two cones beyond that anticipated and some things might bloat or warp.) Those orange peel bumps flatten down, a pleasant gloss starts to appear, even in the more obscure areas. However, the characteristic soda blush that makes it poetically superior to salt burns away for the most part.

I use only two pounds of soda ash per 30 cubic feet of kiln for a cone 6 firing, and even less (1.75 pounds) for a cone 01 earthenware. The water mix is hot to facilitate the melting of those soda lumps, but I'm not sure it makes a lot of difference for dispersal. The spraying times have varied

49

Watering pot by Barbara Tipton, height 14 inches.

between short 1-second bursts and one as long as 6 seconds. What does happen when one sprays for a long time, or equally with many short bursts placed fairly close together without much oxidised relief, is that a reducing atmosphere nearly always takes place regardless of damper position. This certainly can be the water's effect, and most useful in industry for the bluing of red brick (see P.W. Beug's paper on this: *(13) The Use of Controlled Atmospheres*, care of Department of Water, Glass and Ceramics, The Royal Danish Technical University, Copenhagen, Denmark).

I used to close the dampers as much as I could get away with. The idea was traditional in that most of the vapour could be collected – like in a balloon, but continuously – and then persuaded to circulate on its way out. With soda, though, no circulation, no distribution and lots of dry pots. I now leave the damper approximately half way open. The air/flame currents are sufficiently active and the results are quite acceptable.

I don't wad the bottom of pots.

Alumina hydrate is sprinkled onto kiln shelves and pots placed on top. When unloading, the alumina is poured off the shelf onto newspaper, sieved through a 40s mesh and re-used next time. The shelves stay totally free of shards this way and have negligible build-up even after 70 firings. Minor erosion of the underneath shelf surface and edges takes place; nothing that a carborundum stone or a stiff wire brush can't take care of easily.

Sometimes I don't care to see glaze in certain areas. This is where I use a slip containing a small amount of alumina hydrate as a resist.

Jack Doherty

Jack Doherty throws his pots using porcelain clay to the surface of which he adds coloured and textured clays and continues to throw so the dynamics of the wheel move and stretch the coloured clays on the surface of the pot to form the decoration. The soda firing enhances and develops the decoration.

Jack fires to 1100°C before beginning a slight reduction. Using the damper at 15 minute intervals, he reduces heavily for 15 minutes. When cone 8 starts to bend, the gas pressure is reduced to stabilise the temperature climb and he begins spraying into the kiln ports.

He uses a solution of 1 lb ($\frac{1}{2}$ kg) of bicarbonate of soda dissolved in 3 litres of hot water. He sprays in 2–3 lb ($1\frac{1}{2}$ kg) of bicarbonate over a 2–2$\frac{1}{2}$ hour period. When cone 9 is bending, the gas pressure is increased and the firing continues until cone 10 is flat. A 20 minute soak is maintained at the end before crash cooling the kiln to 900°C.

Porcelain bowl with an on-layed decoration by Jack Doherty.

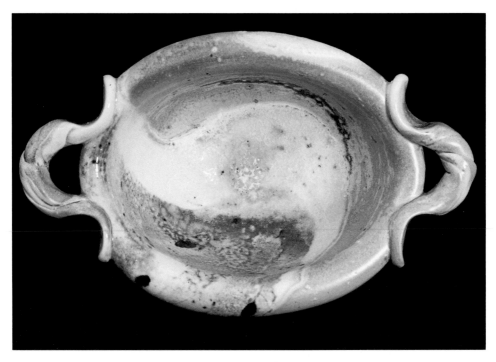

Porcelain dish with handles 22 cm × 10 cm
by Jack Doherty.

Below
Martin Goerg's kiln and burners.

Martin Goerg

Martin Goerg who lives and works in the heart of salt glazing country in Hohr-Grenzhausen, Germany, initially turned to soda glazing because of concern for the environment. He has two spheres of work, thrown domestic ware and one-off large coiled vessels decorated with overlaid slips which are brushed, wiped away and sponged to achieve a textural decoration.

In a $1\,m^3$ downdraught propane-fired kiln, Martin has installed four specially-made atmospheric burners with a tube fitted through a hole into the centre of the burners through which he can spray soda. The kiln is built of light bricks covered with a rough, fire resistant cement wash.

The kiln is fired with a reduced atmosphere up to about 1230–1250°C;

Vessel with multiple slips by Martin Goerg.

then soda glazing starts. Sodium carbonate is mixed 1 : 10 with water (500–700 g soda: 5–7 litres water) and put into a pressurised tank (up to 3-bar pressure) and then injected through the hole in the burners into the kiln chamber. It takes him 15–30 minutes to introduce the soda into the kiln. The firing finishes at 1230–1250°C.

Soda's tendency not to circulate aggressively to every corner of the kiln allows different colours to develop on the vessels, and Martin sets pieces into the kiln to take advantage of this. He particularly likes using china clay/ball clay slips which develop oranges and pinks when coming into contact with only a small amount of soda vapour.

Martin Goerg uses china clay/ball clay slips to develop oranges and pinks.

Jay Lacouture

Jay Lacouture who lives and works in Rhode Island, USA, ascribes to the admittedly romantic but apt words of poet/philosopher Kahlil Gibran: 'Your pots are not your pots... They come through you but not from you... You can give them your love but not your thoughts.' His choice to make functional pots is part of this set of beliefs. 'Although my pots are certainly a reflection of me, they are, more importantly, a reflection of themselves. They complete their mission when they are used and enjoyed by someone.'

Trying to achieve the appropriate marriage of form and surface is an important concern for Jay.

The dramatic effect of soda vapor glazing helps to demonstrate the power of the fire and the nuance of form and surface. Rather than look for a uniform surface, I prefer a more dramatic sense that gives each piece a variety of color and tactile qualities. This 'bizen-like' approach sometimes

Porcelain teapot with thick slip decoration $9 \times 5\frac{1}{2} \times 7$ in. by Jay Lacouture.

Left
Porcelain vase with slip decoration 22½ in.
high by Jay Lacouture.

Above
Porcelain pitcher by Jay Lacouture,
8 × 4½ × 7½ in.

necessitates re-firing and re-positioning pieces in the kiln. After many firings in the same kiln, I have become aware of the 'hot spots' and choose certain pieces to position strategically in certain spots.

He fires a 30 cu.ft. downdraught kiln with a hardbrick interior and soft brick exterior. The exterior of the hardbrick arch is coated with a 5 in (13 cm) layer of castable refractory (see recipe in Appendix 1). The kiln has two ports for blowing the soda ash and sawdust in at the front.

After preheating the kiln overnight, he fires to around cone 4 (1168–1186°C Standard Orton Cone) in an oxidation atmosphere. There is no body reduction as he uses porcelain and prefers the colour of the glazes to be more vibrant. The only reduction is achieved when the damper is closed slightly when he adds the mixture of soda ash and sawdust to the kiln.

At cone 5 (1177–1196°C) he begins to add this mixture using a blower system. Apart from the blower itself, the materials for the apparatus are inexpensive and readily available. He mixes about 1 lb ($\frac{1}{2}$ kg) of soda ash to two gallons of coarse sawdust. This mixture is added to the two gallon hopper and subsequently blown into each hot firebox. With no additional water added to the soda mixture, the water content in the sawdust not only helps to volatilise the sodium, but the resulting ash circulates in the chamber yielding yet another possibility for enhancing the surfaces of the pots. This procedure is repeated (sometimes adding a little less soda ash) about four times. When cone 8 bends and his porcelain body is vitrified, the last bit of soda/sawdust is added and the kiln is shut down.

A thick textural slip is applied to the pots in anticipation of the generosity of the vapour glazing. Jay's slips are mixed with one tablespoon of Calgon to one cup of water to deflocculate the slip (making it more fluid with less water) so it is possible to apply the slip very thickly.

I rely on the slip for both its visual and its tactile appeal. For me, this surface quality is the closest thing to a fresh wet pot. I like to think of these pots as 'beings'. Our culture tends to dismiss inanimate objects as soulless things. Any object that has so much of its maker's will and aspirations in it transcends the world of ordinary things and enters a world of 'being'. Each time I sit at the wheel, I can only hope that the elusive moment of 'being' will present itself and that I might be sensitive enough to recognise it and fortunate enough to be part of it.

Val Nicholls

Val lives and works in Tasmania, Australia. She sieves a mixture of sodium bicarbonate 5 lb (2.5 kg) and borax $1\frac{1}{2}$ lb (250 g) twice through a 120s mesh before dissolving them in 10 litres of hot water. As cone 8 is bending, the damper is adjusted to ensure a light reduction atmosphere, and the gas pressure is turned down to 60–70 kph from about 90–100 kph.

The sodium mixture is heated to boiling point and decanted into a small garden sprayer, and the soda is sprayed into the chamber for a count of 10. The damper is then quickly pushed down completely or 'flapped' for a count of 5 to create turbulence. The procedure is repeated for about two hours or until the test rings indicate that there is sufficient soda on the ware.

When spraying is complete, the burners are turned up to gain heat, and once cone 10 is bending, the kiln is soaked for 30 minutes to one hour. At the end of the firing all ports are opened and the kiln is fast cooled to 1000°C before it is clammed up and left to cool.

Left
Jug by Val Nicholls, 15 cm high.

Above
Val Nicholls jar form, faceted, 24 cm high.

Gail Nichols

Gail Nichols is an American who lives and works in New South Wales, Australia. After salt glazing as a student, she realised that living in metropolitan Sydney meant she had to find an alternative method of glazing.

The inspiration for her work comes from primitive artists around the world, especially Aboriginal and African art. 'Inspiration for my work has also come largely from the lines and imagery of the Australian bush. The elegant twisted curves of the Eucalyptus, adopting almost human forms and the reflection of these lines and forms in Aboriginal art...'

Gail has developed a soda mix of 50/50 soda bicarbonate and soda ash.

These are mixed with an equal amount of calcium carbonate which serves to separate the soda particles and prevent them from setting in a lump in the firebox. Water is added to the mixture to make a 'soupy' consistency. This mixture is stirred constantly until it begins to get warm and to set (a bit like mixing plaster). Rubber gloves are required at all stages of handling to protect hands from the alkaline mixture. As it starts to harden, it is broken up into small pieces, and on a length of angle iron about 8 lb (4 kg) of dry mix processed in this way is scooped at intervals into the fireboxes through the ports above the burners of her 17 cu.ft. LPG (Liquid Petroleum Gas) fired kiln.

The calcium carbonate serves to disperse the soda material, helping it to

volatilise and preventing it from melting into a lump in the firebox. It also helps to protect the lining of the firebox. The water, which chemically combines with the mixture, is released as water vapour into the kiln (without the use of a spray apparatus), and assists in distributing the soda vapour through the kiln. The soda ash is essential as it is responsible for the setting of the wet mixture into a solid which can be broken up and placed in the firebox.

Immediately after firing there is a lump of material (calcium carbonate and some partly fused soda) in each firebox. If you wait for a couple of weeks before trying to remove it, the lump will have softened to a powder which can easily be scooped out of the firebox. Gail puts this mixture through a garden sieve to remove the large chunks and then uses it again as 50% of the mixture for the next firing (with 50% fresh calcium carbonate) in the soda mix recipe.

The firing from raw to glazed lasts about 18 hours. As the bisque stage is completed, the kiln is reduced for 2–3 hours. Putting the soda into the kiln takes about an hour, starting when cone 8 is bending and maintaining that temperature and an oxidising atmosphere. After the soda is finished, she uses a combination of temperature increase and soaking periods to bring cone 10 down.

Her slips have a high alumina: silica ratio based on china clay rather than ball clay with some added colourants

Left
Gail Nichols' platter 48 cm diameter.
Photograph by Ian Whatman

Right
Cylindrical form with iron, rutile, cobalt slips, 90 cm high by Gail Nichols.
Photograph by Ian Whatman

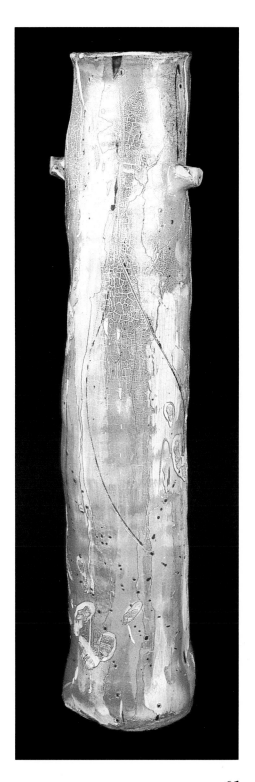

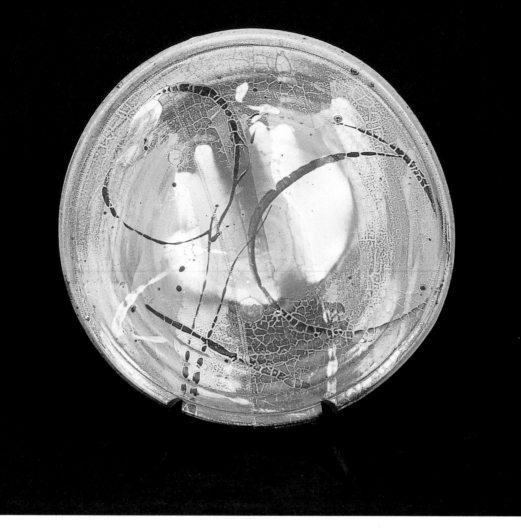

Platter, stoneware with iron, cobalt, rutile slips and manganese brushed 41 cm diameter by Gail Nichols.   *Photograph by Ian Whatman*

such as cobalt used in moderation: orange = pure kaolin, apricot = rutile slip, bright blue = cobalt, iridescent green = cobalt + rutile, all with an addition of 10% bentonite.

The most important advice I could give to potters interested in soda firing is: EXPERIMENT. Try different clay bodies, experiment with slip recipes and ways of applying slips. Be creative in packing the kiln; stack pots on one another; use one pot to shade another

from the soda vapour and create flashings; use a few strategically placed saggar bricks or pieces of kiln shelves to direct the flame and vapour. Use your imagination. There is no right or wrong technique. Listen to other potters for advice, but don't believe them when they say something won't work. Try it yourself first. Most of all: try to avoid making 'imitation salt glaze' pots. Soda glaze is an exciting process in its own right.

Radcliffe College Ceramics Studio

Warren Mather's 'Reading Matter', cone 10, stoneware, soda vapour glazed, $10 \times 15 \times 12$ in.

The Radcliffe Ceramics Studio in Massachusetts, USA, is where Warren Mather and Bernice Hillman started soda glazing back in the 1970s, and Warren Mather is still the guru of soda there today. The school provides the opportunity for study in all areas of ceramics for a diverse group of undergraduate and postgraduate students, professional potters, members of the public wishing to continue ceramic studies, and a staff with a broad range of aesthetic, cultural and technical interests. Mima Weissmann, a member of the staff there doing advanced study, explains the methods used by many at Radcliffe.

> The kiln at Radcliffe is 36 cu.ft. soft brick with hard brick framing the spray ports which are built into the sides and back of the kiln. The door is built up each time the kiln is packed and fired providing flexibility in the number of spray ports built into the door.

Above
'Bud vases' by Mima Weissmann, $2\frac{1}{2}$–$4\frac{1}{2}$ in. high.

Below
Wayne Fuerst spraying into kiln at Radcliffe Ceramics Studio.

The students have learned to adapt the clay bodies to achieve different effects from the soda. Silica sand is added to enhance the orange-peel effect. Adding a small amount of porcelain to a stoneware body gives a more satiny surface.

Different solutions of soda ash are used by each participant. Mima Weissmann fires to cone 9/10 and packs the kiln tightly, which helps to achieve a variety of surfaces and flashing. She uses a solution of $2\frac{1}{2}$ pounds of soda ash to 5 gallons of water and usually does not use all of the solution. Instead of introducing the soda vapour into the kiln at cone 7, 'we have found that beginning spray rounds when cone 9 begins to fall still gives us enough time to complete the rounds before the kiln reaches temperature'.

I spray rounds of 15 seconds into the front and side ports and 20 to 30 seconds into each of the two rear ports using almost all of the solution.

Mima Weissmann plate, brown/white stoneware with impressed pattern and porcelain inlay, $7\frac{1}{2}$ in. diameter.

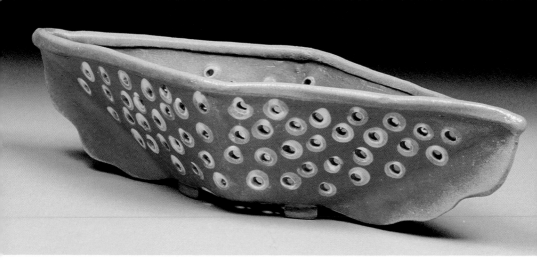

Above
Terry Hass slab-built colander, stoneware.
Radcliffe Ceramics Studio.

Below
Frog dish by Amy Woods, 9 × 7 × 5 in.
Radcliffe Ceramics Studio.

Other potters use only 3 gallons of water and pack the kiln less tightly. The gas and air may be turned down, the damper may be opened or closed a few inches while spraying. When firing stoneware, I try for a gentle body reduction lasting 20–30 minutes at cone 06. A soaking period at the end of the firing seems to enhance the soda effects. Firing time is usually 12–13 hours.

Soda firing like wood firing is labor-intensive and best done with other people, which is one reason why I enjoy this method of firing.

It takes a number of firings to understand the numerous effects that can be achieved. To get a decent plate, for instance, you need maybe a 2-inch space over the plate. Consider the shape of the piece when loading and stacking. It is important to keep the wand of the sprayer moving while spraying to avoid building up the solution on the bottoms of the shelves which can collect there and drip onto work below. Sometimes when a piece

Susan Peterson's 'Sarcophagus', 11 × 10 × 12 in. Radcliffe Ceramics Studio.

is placed in a protected area, the surface is more dry, but you can achieve good flashing effects. Each firing is different depending on how the kiln has been stacked. There are always surprises from this exciting method of firing.

Amy Wood decorates her work out of cone 3 to cone 6 stoneware and decorates with underglazes and slips before biscuit firing to cone 3. This temperature is low enough to keep the red colour of the clay, yet high enough to vitrify the body. The pieces are fired a second time in a cone 1 oxidation atmosphere soda firing to give a dull sheen to some of the clay surfaces. In the areas where she wants the slips to be particularly shiny she sprays a little frit added to some underglaze. To get the patterns with the red clay body showing,

Lobster coffee set by Kathi Thompson, porcelain, 15 in. high, fired to cone 10.

Amy uses templates made of clay laid on the surface of the piece during the firing. The areas which are covered stay lighter and less shiny than the rest.

Phil Rogers

Known more for his ash glazes and salt glazing, Phil from Rhayader, Wales, has done some experimenting with soda glazing. In an Olsen fast fire-type wood-fired kiln, he sprays the soda into the fireboxes as cone 10 is well over. On the pot illustrated here he brushed slip made of $\frac{1}{3}$ Molochite to $\frac{2}{3}$ SMD ball clay, and then after the biscuit firing, the pot was dipped into another slip, milk thin, of 2000 parts of porcelain clay to 700 parts of china clay. The inside is glazed with an ash glaze.

Stoneware jar by Phil Rogers, 15 in. high.

Chris Staley

Chris Staley teaches at Pennsylvania State University, USA. Although he now uses salt when he vapour fires, when he was a student he started using soda ash. He put it into the kiln by filling a tube 1 in (2.5 cm) in diameter, then blew the soda into the kiln with a compressor. Later he used half salt and half soda, putting the mixture into the kiln with an angle iron into the firebox. He says that he felt the soda, at times, helped give the copper blues more brilliance. He always uses a combination of glazes and slips.

The fire and the transforming process that happens when the pots are fired are truly magical. The reason I've used soda and salt is because they give an added depth and subtle richness of variation to both glazes and slips. Using small amounts gives me the results I'm after.

Chris Staley porcelain covered jar, 16 in. high, slip and glaze decorated, soda and salt glazed.

Lobster coffee set with Helix Copper Satin green glaze, porcelain by Kathi R. Thompson.

Above
Teapot, faceted and decorated with black slip and rutile trailed, 17 cm high, by Ruthanne Tudball.

Right
Spouted jug, faceted with orange slip and willow ash brushed on top, 32 cm high by Ruthanne Tudball.

Kathi Thompson

After many experiments with putting packets of 2–3 tablespoons of soda wrapped in paper towels and spraying with an insecticide sprayer that continually got clogged, Kathi settled on spraying the powder of bicarbonate of soda into her kiln with a potato sprayer (agricultural use is to spray pesticide and insecticide powders). She uses about 2 cups of soda in a kiln with 22 cu.ft. packing space and none of the mixture ends up on the floor of the fireboxes as clinker. At the end of the firing the kiln is reduced fairly heavily for 10 minutes and then oxidised for 15 minutes before the kiln is shut down and left to cool. This produces very distinct orange flashing and reduced glazes.

Kathi, who is from the south shore of Nova Scotia, Canada is inspired by the sea and all that it contains. She uses a porcellanous stoneware firing to cones 9–10. Using copper glazes, some of which have a barium base, she relies on the interaction of soda with the glazes and bare clay, which flashes orange, for her palette. The glazes react with the soda, producing speckling and gradations of colour.

Kathi's kiln is a 50 cu.ft. gas kiln (with 22 cu.ft. packing space). She has built it with high alumina soft bricks (G–28 by A.P. Green Refractories), and it fires efficiently and evenly.

Ruthanne Tudball

Although I live in England now, I was born and brought up in Southern California in the foothills overlooking the Los Angeles Basin. I have been aware of air pollution since I could draw breath. Initially it was environmental concerns which attracted me to using soda over salt.

Soda glazing my pots is the perfect vehicle for emphasising the making process, which is very important to me. Vapour firing emphasises every finger mark made on the clay and the history of the making of the piece is meticulously recorded by the vapour. I aim to retain as much of the fluid quality of the clay as possible and to return to the user that same tactile experience through handling. Details of my firing process can be found in the chapter on kilns and firing.

I draw inspiration from tide patterns left in sand that show how the water has rearranged the grains to match the rhythm of its movement. There is an inspiring parallel between the sand patterns as indications of global rhythms at work and the clay spinning on the potter's wheel with hands rhythmically moving over the surface as they form the vessel.

I use simple slips into which I either dip leatherhard pots or which I brush on when the pots are on the wheel having just been thrown. I often use an ash glaze brushed or trailed onto the pots. The pots are all raw fired.

Appendix 1:
Soda slip tests

From the 'Salt and Soda Weekend' at the Royal Forest of Dean College, Gloucestershire, England, April 1993. The weekend included demonstrations by myself and Jack Doherty plus salt and soda kiln firings.

In the firings were hundreds of extruded test pieces made by students of the college. There were eight different clay bodies used and seven base slips to which ten different colour additions were made. Two sets of the test pieces were made for firing in a salt kiln and a soda kiln to be compared, discussed and explored by the potters attending the weekend and a panel of salt glaze potters including Mick Casson, Walter Keeler, Peter Starkey, Micki Schloessingk and others with Ruthanne Tudball and Jack Doherty representing soda glazers. It was a lively debate which ended with salt and soda glazers going away with their horizons widened and an acknowledged respect for contemporary vapour glazing in all of its guises.

Below is the information on the tests carried out. In the photographs I have chosen colouring additions 1, 2, 5, and 9 in each slip base and on each of the clay bodies.

Jack Doherty stains (added to porcelain slips)

Dark Brown Stain (939) use	7%	*Black Stain* use	7%
Chrome Oxide	25	Chrome	50
Iron Oxide	25	Cobalt	20
Manganese Dioxide	10	Alumina	50
Alumina	40	Iron	60
		Manganese	30

Soft Green Stain use	7%	*Pale Blue (H.F. Colours*	
China clay	40	*Northern Ireland)*	4%
Flint	35	Salmon Stain (Deancraft)	1
Iron	8	Yellow Stain	5
Chrome	16	Rutile	3
Cobalt	2	Orange Stain	4
Copper Carbonate	2	Blue Stain + 1% Rutile	5

Salt and Soda Weekend

Body recipes
Jack Doherty slip recipes

Black Clay
(Harold McWhinnie)
China Clay 40
Ball Clay 30
Flint 5
Red Iron Oxide 15
Manganese Carbonate 10

Talc Body
(Ian Pirie)
Hyplas 71 40
China Clay 40
Talc 20
Fine Molochite 18

White Stoneware
(Andy Holden)
Ball Clay HVAR 50
Ball clay BBV 25
China Clay 25
Sand 10

Teapot by Christopher Staley. Thrown porcelain, soda-glazed, cone 8. 12 inches high.

Salt and soda weekend slip tests

| | Colouring Additions | | | | | | | | | |
SLIP BASE	1	2	3	4	5	6	7	8	9	10
China clay 80 Whiting 40 Feldspar 20	Iron 2	Iron 4	Cobalt 0.5 + Chrome 1	Iron Chromate 3	Base	Mazarine Blue Stain 10	Blythe Red Stain 10	Lime Green Stain 10	Black Stain 10	Mandarin Stain 10
Feldspar 25 China clay 25 Ball clay 25 Quartz 25 Borax frit 3.5	Iron 2	Iron 4	Cobalt 0.5 + Chrome 1	Iron Chromate 3	Base	Mazarine Blue 10 Stain	Blythe Red Stain 10	Lime Green Stain 10	Black Stain 10	Mandarin Stain 10
Ball clay 50 China clay 50	Iron 2	Iron 4	Cobalt 0.5 + Chrome 1	Iron Chromate 3	Base	Mazarine Blue Stain 10	Blythe Red Stain 10	Lime Green Stain 10	Black Stain 10	Mandarin Stain 10
China clay 50 Ball clay 50 Rutile 20 Nepheline syenite 30	Iron 2	Iron 4	Cobalt 0.5 + Chrome 1	Iron Chromate 3	Base	Mazarine Blue Stain 10	Blythe Red Stain 10	Lime Green Stain 10	Black Stain 10	Mandarin Stain 10
China clay 18 Ball clay 20 Flint 25 Nepheline syenite 30 Borax frit 7	Iron 2	Iron 4	Cobalt 0.5 + Chrome 1	Iron Chromate 3	Base	Mazarine Blue Stain 10	Blythe Red Stain 10	Lime Green Stain 10	Black Stain 10	Mandarin Stain 10
On Biscuit Only Feldspar 60 China clay 40	Iron 2	Iron 4	Cobalt 0.5 + Chrome 1	Iron Chromate	Base	Mazarine Blue Stain 10	Blythe Red Stain 10	Lime Green Stain 10	Black Stain 10	Mandarin Stain 10
Porcelain clay	Blue Stain 5 Rutile 1	Black 7 Stain	Yellow Stain 5	Lilac Stain 5	Soft Green Stain 7	Rutile 3	Orange Stain 4	Dark Brown 7	Salmon Stain 1	Pale Blue Stain 4

Clay Codes
1. White stoneware
2. High Iron
3. Buff (ASW/G)
4. Buff and Grog
5. Black Body
6. Talc Body
7. Wad Black (saggar Marl)
8. H.F. Porcelain

Glaze tests (overleaf) are numbered with the clay body number first then the slip code. e.g.: 1A1 is white stoneware with slip A plus 2% iron oxide.

1. White Stoneware

2. High Iron Body

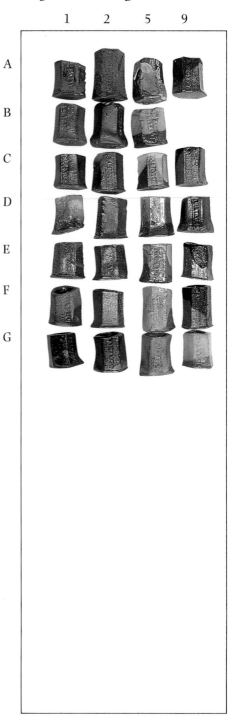

Porcelain slip

3. Buff Stoneware

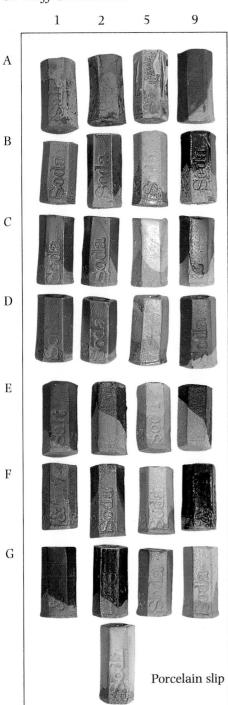

Porcelain slip

4. Buff and Grog

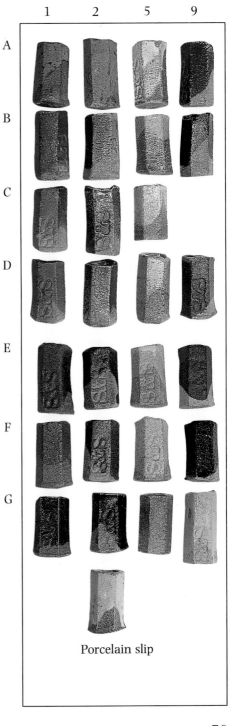

Porcelain slip

Teapot by Margaret Bohls.

Mug by Wayne Fuerst
Radcliffe Ceramics Studio.

Box, 6 cm diameter, by Ruthanne Tudball.

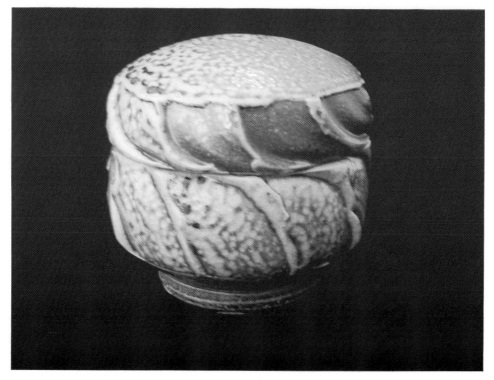

5. Black Body

6. Talc Body

7. Wad Black

	1	2	5	9
A				
B				
C				
D				
E				
F				
G				

Porcelain slip

8. H.F. Porcelain
(Harry Fraser Porcelain)

Appendix 2:
Slip and Glaze Recipes

FROM MARGARET BOHLS
CONE 10 GLAZES FOR OXIDATION SODA FIRING

WOO BASE: Satin matt

Kona F-4 Feldspar	33 parts
Dolomite	12
Barium carbonate	25
EPK (Kaolin)	7
Flint	7
Zircopax (Ultrox)	15

WOO BLUE (periwinkle)

| add cobalt carbonate | 1% |
| rutile | 4% |

WOO WHITE (warm white)   4%
add rutile

WOO PURPLE (maroon, speckled)   4%
add manganese

YELLOW/AMBER (shiny, opaque)

Custer Feldspar	29 parts
Whiting	20.5
EPK	19
Flint	31.5
add Rutile	7%

Bright yellow in oxidation, amber in reduction.

PINK SHINO (shiny, opaque)

Nepheline syenite	48 parts
Spodumene	25
EPK	5
Ball clay	8
Soda feldspar	7
Soda ash	4
add Pink Mason Stain No. 6020	3–8%

ANDY MARTIN SHOWSAVER CHARTREUSE (Shiny, transparent, runs)

Barium carbonate	22.89 parts
Gerstley borate	3.84
Strontium carbonate	12.98
Wollastonite	3.37
Nepheline syenite	26.92
Ball clay	9.52
Flint	20.48
add Chrome	0.5%

REITZ SATIN MATT BLUE

Custer Feldspar	45 parts
Whiting	20
Kaolin	13
Cornwall stone	22
add Rutile	2%
Cobalt carbonate	0.5%
Red iron oxide	2%

Goes shiny bottle green when hit with soda.

ROB'S GREEN (shiny, transparent)

Cornwall stone	75 parts
Whiting	18
Gerstley borate	5
Barium carbonate	10
add copper carbonate	10%

Dark forest green, sometimes gets yellow crystals or black spots.

MATT LIGHT BLUE/LAVENDER (shiny blue when hit with soda)

Nepheline syenite	34 parts	Grolleg	23
Dolomite	14	Flint	17
Whiting	7	add Cobalt carbonate	2%
Zinc oxide	6		

RANDY'S GREEN

Flint	19.2 parts
Ball clay	12
Whiting	10.5
Zircopax (Ultrox)	9
Dolomite	7.3
Barium carbonate	15
Custer Feldspar	25
Kona F-4 Feldspar	21
add Copper carbonate	6%
Tin oxide	4%

Shiny, sometimes metallic in soda.

BRUILLARDS CHARCOAL BLACK

G200 Feldspar	34 parts
Ball clay	11
Custer Feldspar	24
Dolomite	8
Flint	8
Whiting	4
Zircopax (Ultrox)	2
add Black Mason Stain	4%
Red iron oxide	4%

ORANGE SALT/SODA CLAY BODY *(cone 10)*

Tile 6 (kaolin)	30 parts	
EPK	20	Foundry Hill Stone can be
Goldart	40	substituted for Goldart. Custer
G200 Feldspar	6	Feldspar can be substituted for
Flint	4	G200 Feldspar.

FROM JOHN CHALKE (cone 6)

PALE BLUE SANDY FLAT MATT (I like this against a grey background)

Alumina hydrate (flour grade)	15 parts
6 Tile kaolin	5
Mason Stain Black 6600	1

LIGHT MOSS GREY-GREEN (porous-looking surface)

Alumina hydrate (flour)	15 parts
6 Tile kaolin	10
Chrome oxide	0.5

LIGHT ORANGE

Alumina hydrate (flour grade)	20 parts
6 Tile kaolin	10
Rutile	3

In spite of this apparently being high in rutile, and therefore refractory, it in fact seals rather pleasantly on the edges.

FROM JACK DOHERTY (cone 10)

INTERIOR GLAZE

Talc	23 parts
Feldspar	26
China clay	22
Whiting	13
Flint	22

BODY COLOURS

1. Mid-Brown: Red iron oxide 3%
2. Black:

Chrome	50 gms	
Cobalt	20	
Alumina hydrate	50	Add 10% of this black stain to 3000 g of dry
Iron oxide	60	body.
Manganese	30	

3. Soft Green:

China clay	40 gms	10% of this soft green is added to 3000 g of
Flint	35	dry body.
Feldspar	25	

Iron oxide	8
Chrome	16
Cobalt	2
Copper carbonate	2

4. Speckled grey: Rutile   3%   added to dry body
5. Heavy speckle: Ilmenite   3%   added to dry body

All of the oxide combinations and stains are added to crushed dry body, reconstituted and stored for a few weeks before use.

BATT WASH AND KILN WASH

Ball clay	1 part
Alumina	3 parts

FROM MARTIN GOERG (cone 6–7)

WHITE SLIP

China clay	50
Quartz	20
Westerwald clay	30

ORANGE SLIP

China clay	50
Ball clay	50

BLUE SLIP

Westerwald clay	
Cobalt oxide	1.5%

SHINO GLAZE

Nepheline syenite	80
Ball clay	20

FROM JAY LACOUTURE (cone 8)

J'S SALT SLIP

Avery kaolin	25
Grolleg	10
OM4 ball clay	25
Soda spar	15
Whiting	5
Flint	15
Borax	5

(Add 1 tablespoon of Calgon dissolved in one cup of water to the slip while mixing for a thick creamy consistency.)

HELMAR SLIP

Helmar clay	25
Custer Spar	12.5
Flint	26
Pyrotrol	26
Ball clay	3.5
Fireclay	3.5

IRON YELLOW GLAZE

Custer Spar	45 parts
Flint	23
Whiting	17
Kaolin	13
Zinc	2
Red iron	7

BARIUM SEMI

F-4 Spar	40 parts
Barium carbonate	31
Dolomite	12
Kaolin	9
Flint	9
add:	
Copper carbonate	4% (nice blue)
Spanish Iron	6% (rich iron yellow/brown)

KCAI BODY

6 Tile clay	50 parts
OM4 ball clay	10
Custer Spar	25
Flint	20
Pyrotrol	13
Bentonite	4.5

J'S PORCELAIN

Grolleg	60 parts
Custer Spar	19
Flint	17
Pyrotrol	6
Bentonite	3

INSULATING CASTABLE (All measurements by volume)

Fireclay	1 part
Portland cement	1 part
Sand	0.5 part
Coarse sawdust	2 parts
Vermiculite	2 parts

SODIUM RESISTANT CASTABLE

Lumnite cement (high alumina)	1 part
Fireclay	2 parts
Coarse grog (30s–40s) mesh	1 part
Vermiculite	2 parts

FROM VAL NICHOLLS (cone 9–10)

BASE SLIP (can add 10% commercial stains for colour)

Ball clay	50	Light tan, pink, orange blush on white stoneware or
China clay	50	porcelain.

SLIP NO.2

Nepheline syenite	1	This looks good on raw LGH clay. (This is an Australian
Ekalite (kaolin)	1	buff stoneware.)
Ball clay	1	

On a white body: 90% water + 10% oxide e.g. cobalt, copper, chrome or cobalt and copper (50/50).

COPPER SATIN GLAZE

Nepheline syenite	50 parts	
Silica	28	Causes blushing on shinos
Whiting	24	and slips occasionally.
EP kaolin	14	
Bentonite	3	
Copper carbonate	1	
Black copper oxide	5	

FROM GAIL NICHOLS (cone 9–10)

BASIC SLIP FOR SODA GLAZE

Kaolin	80 parts	
Potash feldspar	10	This slip alone gives a white shino-like
Silica	10	surface with some pink/orange flashing.
Bentonite	10	

Additions for colour include:

Red iron oxide	2%	Red/Brown
Rutile	3%	Gold
Rutile with cobalt carbonate	0.3%	Gold/Green
Cobalt carbonate	0.3%	Blue
Manganese dioxide	5%	Brown/Black

HIGH ALUMINA SLIP

Kaolin	100 parts	This slip results in a drier surface and a
Bentonite	10	brilliant orange colour.

SODA MIX

Soda bicarbonate	25 parts
Soda ash	25
Calcite	50

INTERIOR GLAZE

Potash feldspar	20 parts	
Calcite	18	This is a black glaze
Silica	21	used as a raw glaze.
Kaolin	20	
Dolomite	11	
Nepheline syenite	9	
Bentonite	5	
Red iron oxide	2	
Cobalt carbonate	0.5	

FROM RADCLIFFE COLLEGE CERAMICS STUDIO

AMY WOODS BLACK SLIP:

Redart	50 parts
Ball clay	25
Manganese dioxide	15
Black stain	12
Black iron	5

STONE WHITE: (used as liner)

Custer Feldspar	54 parts
Dolomite	18
Whiting	3
EPK	25
Zircopax	10

CARBON TRAP GLAZE:

Kona F-4 Feldspar	35 parts
Spodumene	30
EPK	10
Soda ash	8
Nepheline syenite	15
Ball clay	5
Bentonite	2

BROWN STONEWARE CLAY:

AP Green	40
Tonn base clay no. 9	40
G200 Feldspar	5
Flint (200s mesh)	5
Redart	10
Grog	10

WHITE STONEWARE CLAY:

Goldart	20
EPK	20
XX Saggar clay	20
AP Green	20
Feldspar F-200	10
Flint (200s mesh)	10
Silica sand	2

ORIBE GLAZE:

Custer Feldspar	26.5 parts
Flint (325s mesh)	32.6
EPK	3.1
Talc	3.7
Whiting	16.6
Strontium carbonate	8.7
Bone ash	1.8
Black copper oxide	4.2
Bentonite	2.0

JILL BONOVITZ TERRA SIGILLATA:

Calgon	7.5 g
Bentonite	60.0 g
Edgar Plastic Kaolin	1170.0 g
Kentucky ball clay (OM 4)	270.0 g
	1507.5 g

Mix with 14 cups of water and allow to settle for 24 hours. Slip divides into three layers. Siphon off and discard top watery layer, retain middle layer for base to which colorants can be added.

FROM CHRIS STALEY

For the early glazes with blues and greens I used the two following glazes by means of dipping and careful spraying on porcelain:

ROB'S GREEN

Cornwall stone	7500 g
Whiting	1800 g
Colemanite	500 g
Copper carbonate	1000 g
Barium carbonate	1000 g
Bentonite	200 g

STALEY'S RED TO GREEN

Custer Feldspar	50 parts
Whiting	15
EPK kaolin	13
Dolomite	2
Flint	20
Copper carbonate	8
Iron oxide	1
Bentonite	2%

RUTILE SLIP: *Yellow*

Custer Feldspar	10.5 g
Talc	10.5 g
Ball clay	21.0 g
Kaolin	32.6 g
Silica	26.3 g
Rutile	15.0 g

FROM KATHI R. THOMPSON (cone 9–10)

HELIX COPPER SATIN

Nepheline syenite	50%	
Flint (silica)	28	This glaze is rather unforgiving
Whiting	24	and is best sprayed on. It is
EPK	14	suitable in light reduction.
add		
Copper carbonate	1	
Black copper oxide	5	
Bentonite	3	

TAZMANIA BLACK *(cone 4–10)*

Gerstley borate	21%	
Wollastonite	8	
Nepheline syenite	30	This suits a broad range of
Kaolin	10	firing temperatures – very
Silica (flint)	31	forgiving, stable glaze.
Black iron oxide	10	
add		
Chrome	2	
Cobalt oxide or carbonate	3	
Manganese dioxide	6	

POSITIVE BLUE

Barium carbonate	36.1%	A somewhat unforgiving and rather
Nepheline syenite	43.7	'persnickety' glaze, but worth
Ball clay	10.9	learning to respect.
Flint (silica)	9.3	
Copper oxide	4.4	It is best sprayed on and suitable
Bentonite	1.1	in light reduction.

FLASHING SLIP

EPK	70%	Interesting slip brushed onto
Nepheline syenite	30	bare clay. Good in reduction.

CLAY BODY (Throwing and Handbuilding)

Tile 6 kaolin	30
Grolleg	10
EPK	10
Ball clay	15
Custer Feldspar	15
Flint	15
Pyrophyllite	5

FROM RUTHANNE TUDBALL (cone 8–10)

ORANGE SLIP

Ball clay (1.5% iron)	50
Grolleg china clay	50

WHITE SLIP

SMD ball clay	50
China clay	50

BLACK SLIP

AT ball clay	33
Porcelain clay powder	33
Soda feldspar	33
add	
*Black stain	15%

*BLACK STAIN

Chrome oxide	54
Red iron oxide	26
Manganese dioxide	44
Cobalt oxide	5

RED SHINO

AT ball clay	33
Nepheline syenite	33
Soda feldspar	33

WILLOW ASH GLAZE:

Raw ash	5 parts
Soda feldspar	5 parts
SMD ball clay	4 parts
Quartz	4 parts
Bentonite	2%

Wadding

Alumina hydrate	3 parts
China clay	1 part

Batt Wash
Same as wadding but mixed to a milky consistency with water.

APPENDIX 3:
Clay analysis (%)
(of clays mentioned in recipes)

	SiO$_2$	Al$_2$O$_3$	Fe$_2$O$_3$	TiO$_2$	CaO	Na$_2$O	K$_2$O	KNaO	S$_2$O$_3$	P$_2$O$_5$	MgO
KAOLINS											
Grolleg	47.7	37.7	0.60	0.03	0.10			1.92			0.25
EPK	46	37.8	0.60	0.40	0.10	0.20	0.25		0.03	0.05	0.15
Tile 6	46.9	38.2	0.35	1.42	0.43	0.04					0.58
BALL CLAYS											
AT	54	29	2.4	1.1	0.30	0.50	3.0				0.40
SMD	63	24	1.1	1.2	0.30	0.40					0.40
Bandy Black XX	61	24.5	0.99	1.3	0.09	0.40	1.7		0.11	0.07	0.12
Saggar	57.4	28.9	0.7	1.7	0.5	0.3	0.9				0.3
STONEWARE CLAYS											
Goldart	57.3	28.5	1.2	1.9	0.08			1.2			0.22
FIRECLAYS											
AP Green	52	30	1.0	1.5	0.05	0.05	0.2				0.03
EARTHENWARE CLAYS											
Redart	54.3	16.4	7.04	1.06	0.23	0.40	4.07		0.24	0.17	1.55
Albany slip:	58	14	5.2	0.8	6.0	0.8	3.25				2.2
Bentonite	64.3	20.7	3.5	0.11	0.45	2.9			0.35		2.3

POTASH FELDSPARS
Custer Feldspar
Cornwall Stone
K-200 Feldspar

SODA FELDSPARS
Kona F/4 Feldspar

LITHIUM FELDSPAR
Spodumene

PYROPHYLLITE
A mineral, actually alumina silicate. Sometimes it is used as a substitute for china clay, although it does not shrink or expand in the same way china clay does. Empirical formula: SiO$_2$ (75.4%); AL$_2$O$_3$ (20.3%); Fe$_2$O$_3$ (0.1%); CaO (0.2%); Na$_2$O (0.2%); H$_2$O (2 or 3%). It is added to clay to reduce thermal shock.

References

Blacker, J.F., *The ABC of English Salt-Glaze Stoneware From Dwight to Doulton*, Stanley Paul & Co., London, 1922.

Kingery, W. David and Pamela B. Vandiver, *Ceramic Masterpieces Art, Structure and Technology*, Collier Macmillan Pub., London, 1986.

Lawrence, W.G. and R.R. West, *Ceramic Science for the Potter*, Chilton Book Company.

Mather, Warren and Bernice Hillman, 'Salt in the City: The Sodium Carbonate Solution,' in *The Studio Potter*, 1978, vol.7, no.1.

Parmelee, Cullen W., *Ceramic Glazes*, revised by Cameron G. Harman, Cahers Pub. Co., Boston, Mass.

Kingzett's Chemical Encyclopedia, Balliere, Tindall and Cassell.

Stevens, R. and J. Cossey, *Boric Oxide as a Constitutent of Salt Glazes*, Borax Consolidated Ltd., Technical Service Bulletin No.10, 1948.

Troy, Jack, 'The Flash Factor', *Ceramics Art and Perception*, issue 15, 1994.

Troy, Jack, *Salt-Glazed Ceramics*, Watson-Guptill, New York, 1977.

Vandiver, Pamela, 'Appendix A: The Manufacture of Faience,' in Kaczmarczyk, A. and R.E.M. Hedges, *Ancient Egyptian Faience*, Aris and Phillips, Warminster, 1983.

Zamek, Jeff, 'Sodium Carbonate Vapor Firing'. Thesis for Graduate School, Alfred University, Alfred, NY, 1974.

Discussions with: Emeritus Professor G. Fowles, University of Reading Chemistry Department, Berkshire, England. Peter Hibbert of British Gas Scientific Services.

Ginger jar by Ruthanne Tudball.

Index